#1 ADULT CONTEMPORARY HITS
OF THE
EIGHTIES

AS LISTED ON THE BILLBOARD ADULT CONTEMPORARY CHARTS

ALL NIGHT LONG
(ALL NIGHT)

Words and Music by
LIONEL RICHIE

Copyright © 1983 Brockman Music (ASCAP)
International Copyright Secured   All Rights Reserved

7

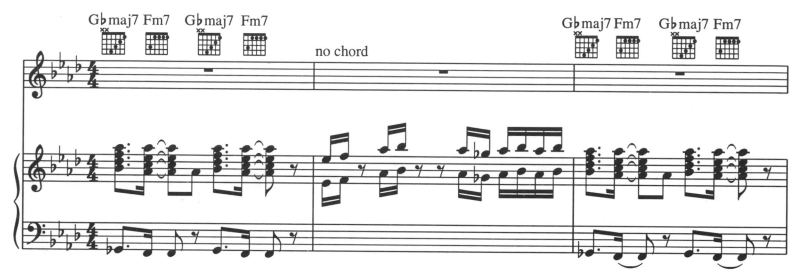

long _____ (All night)   (All night)

Ev - 'ry-one _ you   meet, _   they're jam-ming in _ the   street, _   All night

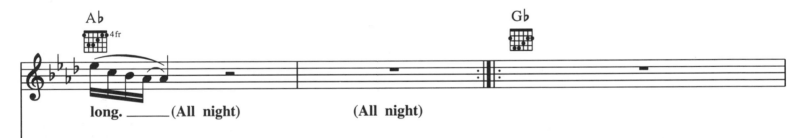

long. _____ (All night)   (All night)

Repeat and Fade

(All night)   (All night)

ANY DAY NOW

Words and Music by BOB HILLIARD
and BURT BACHARACH

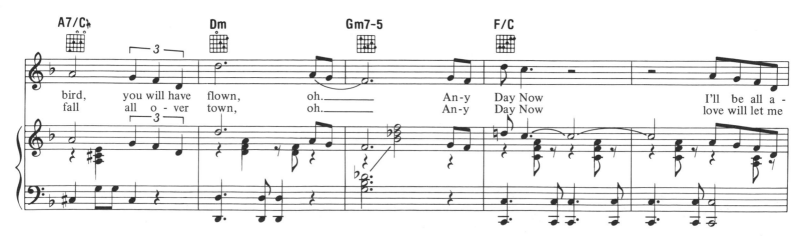

Copyright © 1962 by Unichappell Music Inc.
Copyright Renewed
International Copyright Secured   All Rights Reserved

ALMOST PARADISE
(Love Theme From The Paramount Motion Picture "FOOTLOOSE")

Words by DEAN PITCHFORD
Music by ERIC CARMEN

Moderately Slow

(Male:) I thought that dreams ___ be - longed ___ to
(Male:) It seems like per - fect love's ___ so

oth - er men, ___ 'cause each time I ___ got close ___ they'd
hard to find. ___ I'd al - most giv - en up. ___ You

fall a - part ___ a - gain. ___ (Female:) I feared my heart ___ would beat in ___
must have read ___ my mind. ___ (Female:) And all these dreams ___ I saved for a

Copyright © 1984 by Ensign Music Corporation
International Copyright Secured   All Rights Reserved

AXEL F
(Theme From The Paramount Motion Picture "BEVERLY HILLS COP")

By HAROLD FALTERMEYER

Moderately fast, with a strong beat

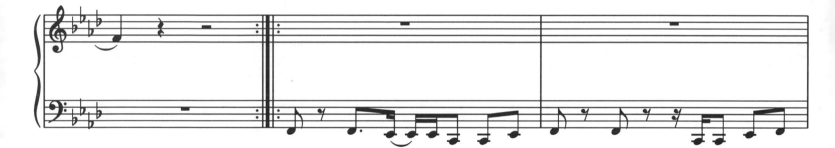

Copyright © 1984, 1985 by Famous Music Corporation
International Copyright Secured   All Rights Reserved

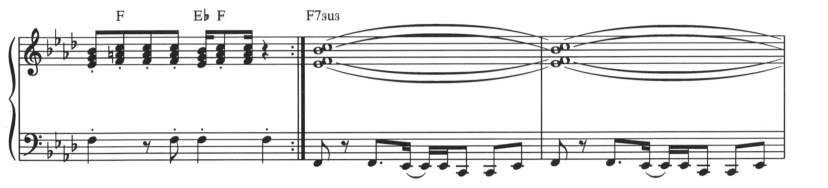

(R.H. 2nd time only)

N.C.

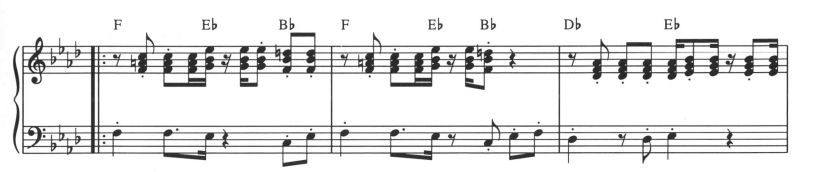

BLUE EYES

Words and Music by ELTON JOHN
and GARY OSBORNE

Blue eyes, ___ ba-by's got blue ___ eyes,
like a deep ___ blue sea ___ on a blue, ___ blue day.
like a clear ___ blue sky ___ watch-ing ov - er me.

Blue eyes, ___ ba-by's got blue ___ eyes,
Blue eyes, ___ ooh, I love blue ___ eyes,

when the morn - ing comes, ___ I'll be far ___ a - way,
when I'm by ___ her side ___ where I long ___ to be, ___

Copyright © 1982 by Big Pig Music Ltd.
All Rights for the United States Administered by Intersong U.S.A., Inc.
International Copyright Secured   All Rights Reserved

CARELESS WHISPER

Words and Music by GEORGE MICHAEL
and ANDREW RIDGELEY

I feel so__ un - sure__
Time can nev - er mend__
To - night the mu - sic seems so loud,__ I

wish that we__ could lose this crowd,
the care - less whis - per
as I take your hand__ and lead you
may - be it's bet - ter this way, if we'd

Copyright © 1984 by Morrison-Leahy Music Ltd.
All Rights for the U.S. Administered by Chappell & Co.
International Copyright Secured   All Rights Reserved

26

should have known bet-ter than to cheat a friend,.and waste a chance that I've.been gi-ven, so I'm nev-er gon-na

dance a-gain_ the way I dance_with you._____

way I dance_with you, oh.___   way I dance_with you._

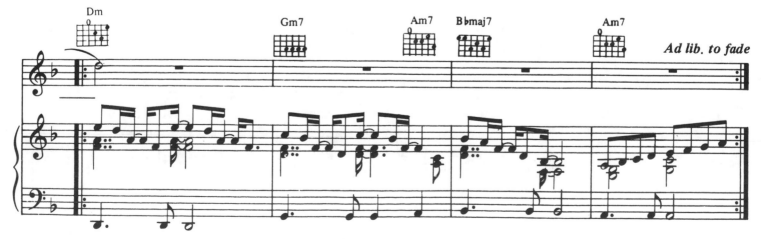

CHARIOTS OF FIRE
(From "CHARIOTS OF FIRE")

Music by
VANGELIS

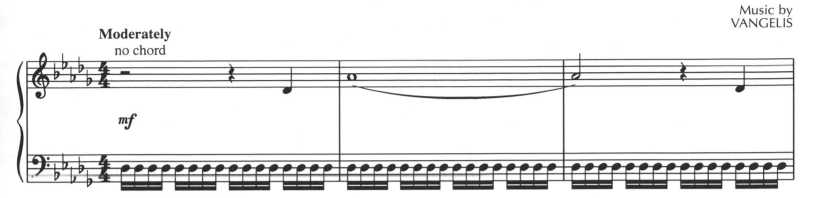

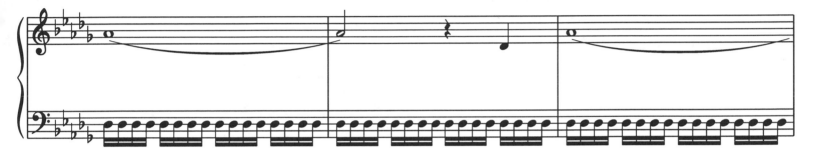

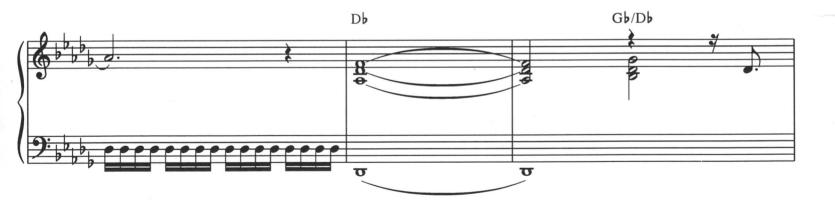

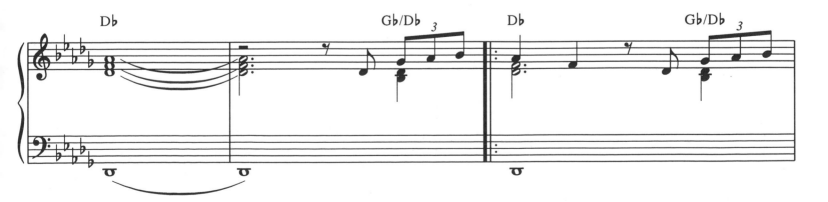

© 1981 EMI MUSIC PUBLISHING LTD.
All Rights for the World, excluding Holland, Controlled and Administered by EMI APRIL MUSIC INC.
All Rights Reserved   International Copyright Secured   Used by Permission

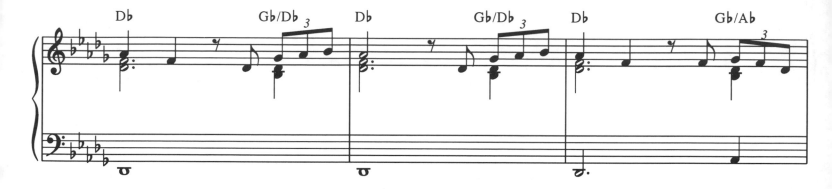

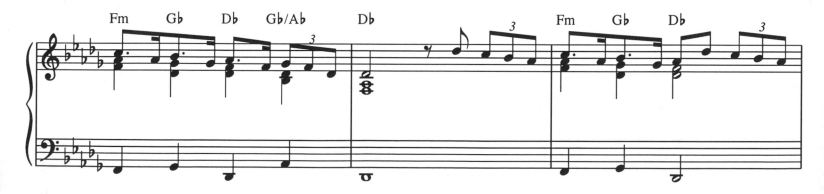

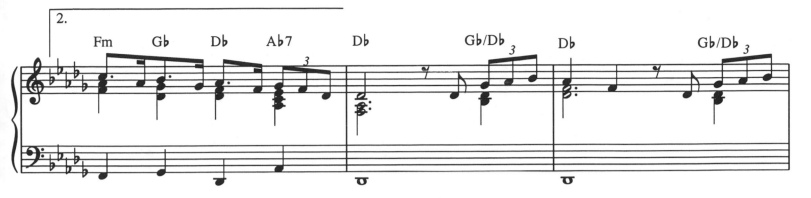

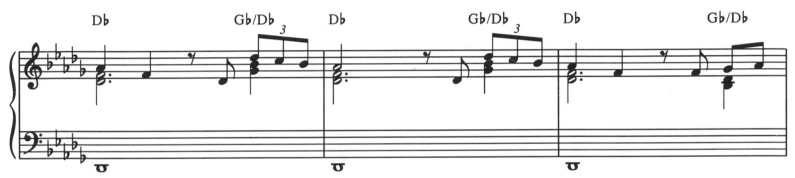
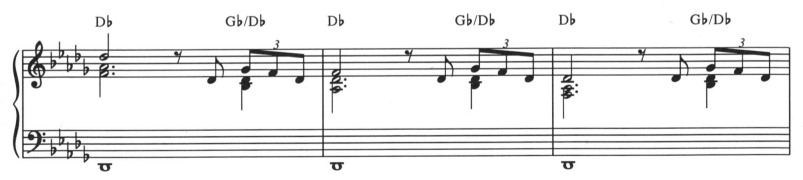
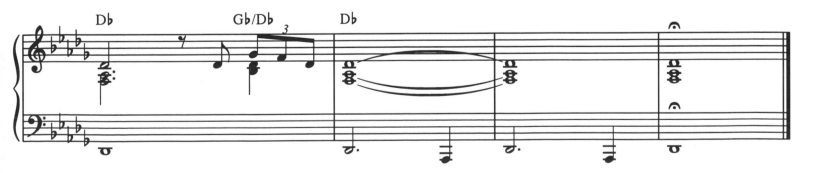

DON'T KNOW MUCH

Words and Music by BARRY MANN, CYNTHIA WEIL
and TOM SNOW

Tenderly

Look at this face, I know the years are show - ing.

Look at this life, _____ I still don't know where_ it's go - ing.

I don't know _____ much, but I know I love you, _____ and

© 1980 ATV MUSIC CORP., MANN & WEIL SONGS, INC., SNOW MUSIC and EMI BLACKWOOD MUSIC INC.
All Rights for ATV MUSIC CORP. and MANN & WEIL SONGS, INC. Controlled and Administered by EMI BLACKWOOD MUSIC INC. under license from ATV MUSIC CORP.
All Rights Reserved   International Copyright Secured   Used by Permission

that may be _____ all I I need to know.

So man - y ques - tions still left un - an - swered.

So much I've nev - er bro - ken through. __

And when I feel you near me some-times I see so clear - ly

ENDLESS LOVE

Words and Music by
LIONEL RICHIE

Copyright © 1981 by PGP Music and Brockman Music
All Rights Administered by Intersong U.S.A., Inc.
International Copyright Secured   All Rights Reserved

ETERNAL FLAME

Words and Music by BILLY STEINBERG, TOM KELLY
and SUSANNA HOFFS

Moderately Steady Beat

Close your eyes, __ give me your hand, __ dar - ling.
I be - lieve __ it's meant to _____ be, ____ dar - ling.

Do you feel __ my heart beat - ing? Do you un - der-stand? __
I watch you when __ you are sleep - ing. You be - long to me. __

Copyright © 1988 Sony Tunes Inc., EMI Blackwood Music Inc. and Bangophile Music
All Rights on behalf of Sony Tunes Inc. Administered by Sony Music Publishing, 8 Music Square West, Nashville, TN 37203
All Rights for Bangophile Music Controlled and Administered by EMI Blackwood Music Inc.
International Copyright Secured   All Rights Reserved

D   Bm7   Am7

2 D

D.S.al Coda

ah.

CODA   D   Bm7   Am7

dream - ing   or   is   this   burn - ing

G   Em7

an   e - ter - nal   flame? ____

Close your eyes. __

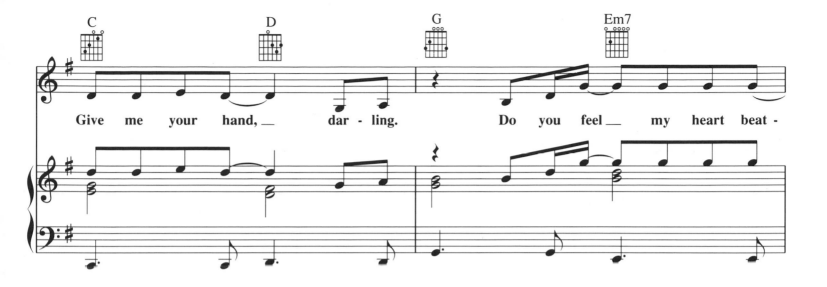

Give me your hand, __ dar - ling. Do you feel __ my heart beat -

- ing? Do you un - der - stand? __ Do you feel the same? __ Am I on - ly

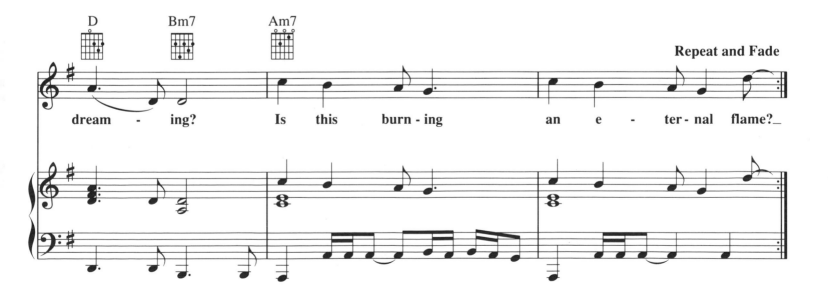

Repeat and Fade

dream - ing? Is this burn - ing an e - ter - nal flame? __

FRIENDS & LOVERS
(BOTH TO EACH OTHER)

Words and Music by PAUL GORDON
and JAY GRUSKA

What would you say if I told you I've al-ways
Yes, it's a chance that we're tak-ing, and some-bod-y's

© 1982, 1986 COLGEMS-EMI MUSIC INC., WB MUSIC CORP. and FRENCH SURF MUSIC
All Rights on behalf of FRENCH SURF MUSIC Administered by WB MUSIC CORP.
All Rights Reserved   International Copyright Secured   Used by Permission

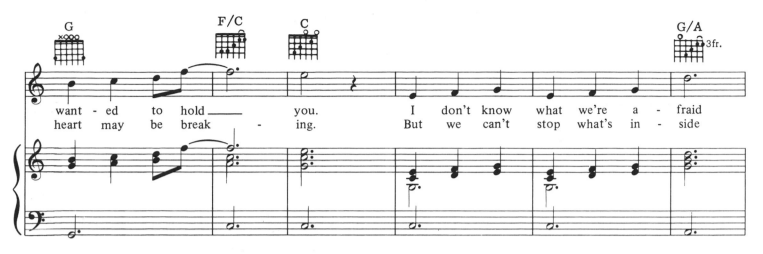

want - ed to hold _____ you. I don't know what we're a - fraid
heart may be break - ing. But we can't stop what's in - side

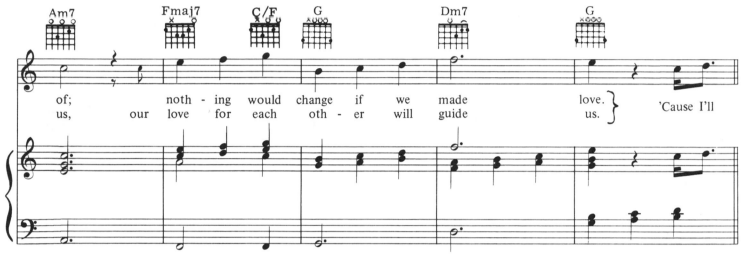

of; noth - ing would change if we made love.
us, our love for each oth - er will guide us. 'Cause I'll

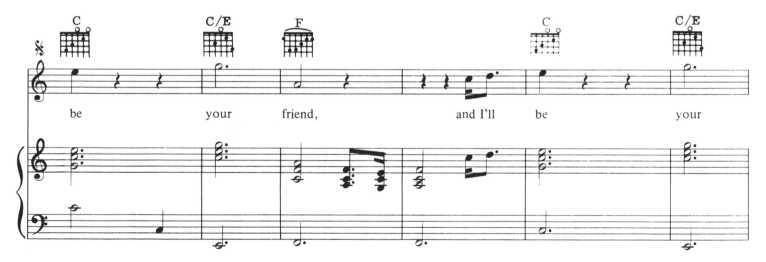

be your friend, and I'll be your

lov - er. Well, I know in our hearts we a - gree _____

we don't have to be one or the oth - er. No,____

____ we could be both to each oth - er.

To Coda

oth - er. I've been through you and you've been through____ me,

some - times a friend____ is the hard - est to

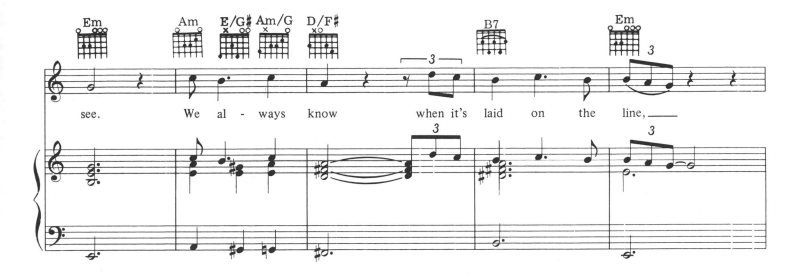

Em   Am E/G# Am/G D/F#   B7   Em

see.   We al - ways know   when it's laid on the line, ___

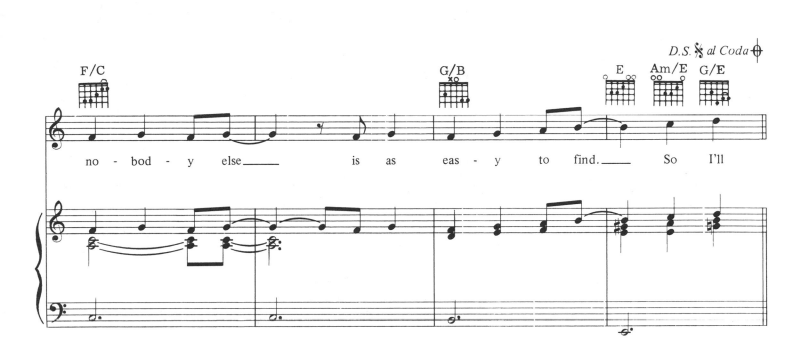

F/C   G/B   E Am/E G/E

no - bod - y else ___ is as eas - y to find.___ So I'll

D.S. 𝄋 *al Coda* ⊕

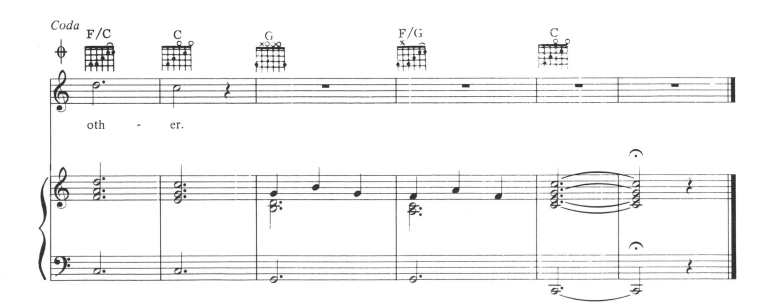

Coda ⊕ F/C   C   G   F/G   C

oth - er.

A GROOVY KIND OF LOVE

Words and Music by TONI WINE
and CAROLE BAYER SAGER

© 1966 (Renewed 1994) SCREEN GEMS-EMI MUSIC INC.
All Rights Reserved   International Copyright Secured   Used by Permission

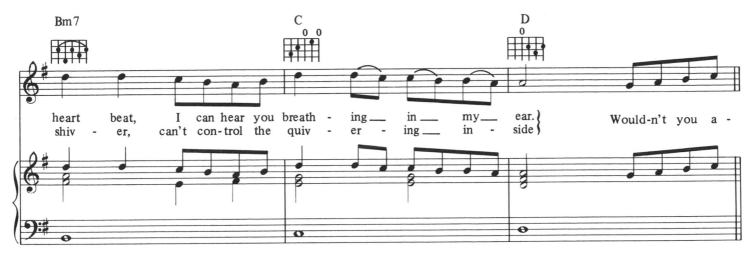

heart beat, I can hear you breath - ing___ in___ my___ ear.
shiv - er, can't con-trol the quiv - er - ing___ in - side }
Would-n't you a -

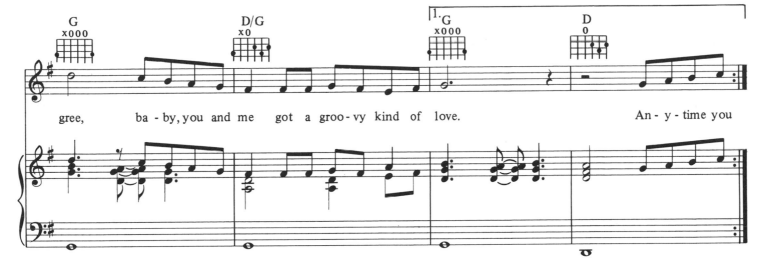

gree, ba-by, you and me got a groo-vy kind of love.
An - y - time you

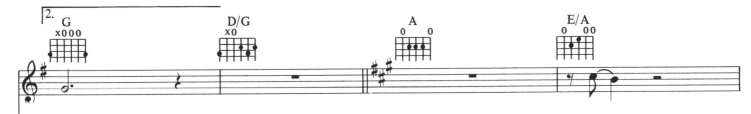

love.
Oh.___

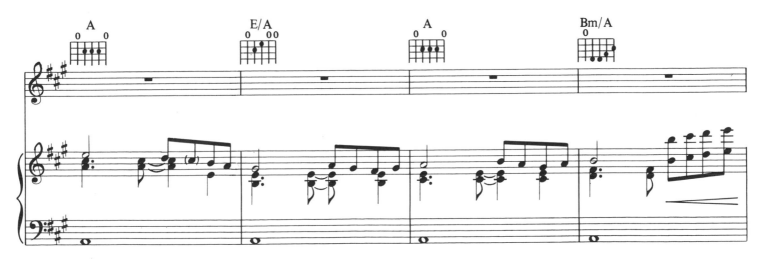

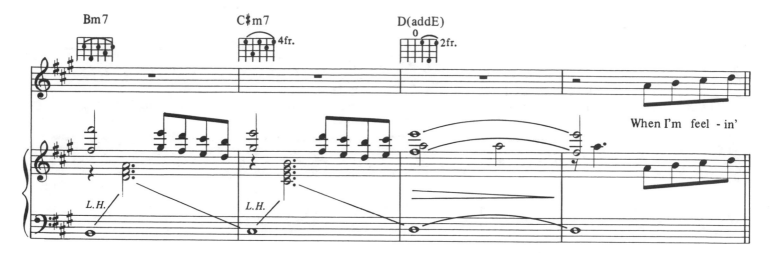

When I'm feel-in'

blue, all I got to do is take a look at you, then I'm not so___

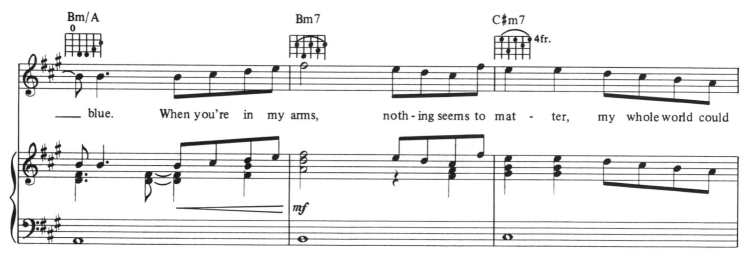

___ blue. When you're in my arms, noth-ing seems to mat-ter, my whole world could

shat - ter, I don't___ care.___ Would-n't you a - gree,___ ba - by, you and

HARD TO SAY I'M SORRY

Words and Music by PETER CETERA
and DAVID FOSTER

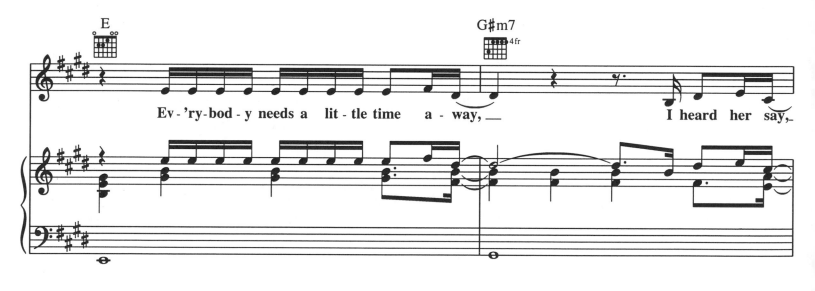

Ev-'ry-bod-y needs a lit-tle time a-way, _____ I heard her say, _____

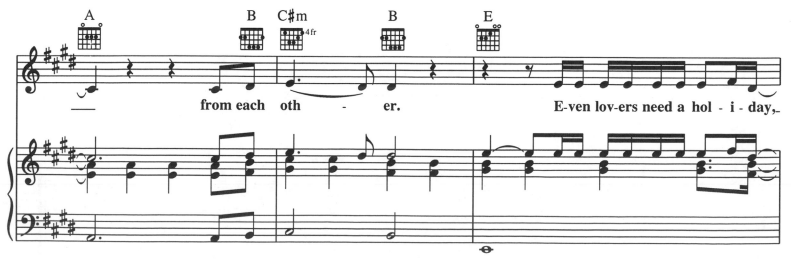

from each oth - er. E-ven lov-ers need a hol-i-day, _____

Copyright © 1982 by BMG Songs, Inc. and Foster Frees Music, Inc.
International Copyright Secured   All Rights Reserved

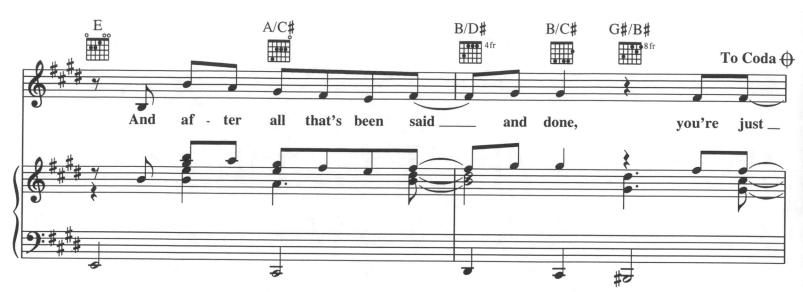

And af-ter all that's been said ___ and done, you're just ___

___ the part ___ of me ___ I can't ___ let go.

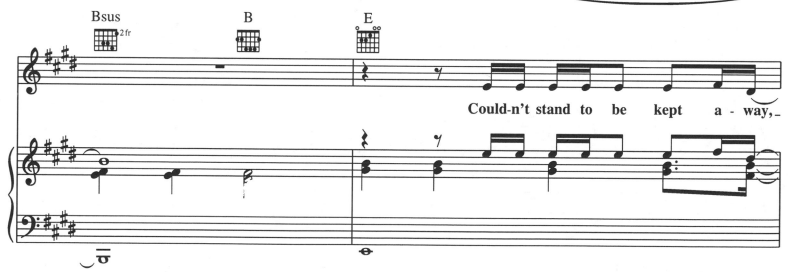

Could-n't stand to be kept a - way, ___

just for the day, ___ from your bod - y.

Hold ____ me now ____ I real-ly want to tell you I'm sor-ry.

I could nev-er let you go.

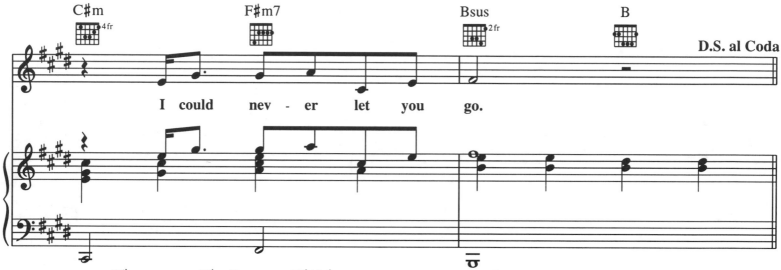

___ the part _ of me _ I can't _ let go.

Af-ter all that we've _ been through, I will make it up _

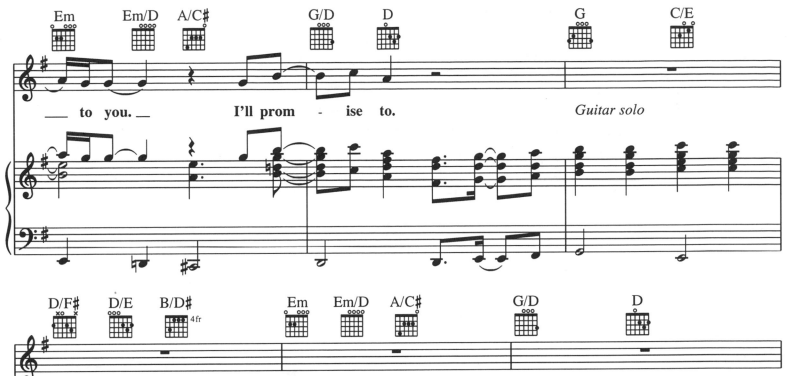

to you. I'll prom - ise to. *Guitar solo*

Solo ends

You're gon-na be _ the luck - y one. _

rall.

HELLO

Words and Music by
LIONEL RICHIE

Copyright © 1983, 1984 Brockman Music (ASCAP)
International Copyright Secured   All Rights Reserved

door _____	Hel - lo,	is it
flow _____	Hel - lo,	I've just
Solo ends	Hel - lo,	is it

me you're look - ing	for?	1. I can see it in your eyes,	I can
got to let you	know,	2.,3. 'Cause I won-der where you are	and I
me you're look - ing	for?		

| see it in your smile | You're all I've ev - er want-ed ____ and my |
| won-der what you do | Are you some - where feel-ing lone - ly ____ or is |

LONGER

Words and Music by
DAN FOGELBERG

Moderate Ballad

Long - er than _ there've been fish - es in the o - cean,
Strong - er than _ an - y moun - tain cath - e - dral.
Through the years _ as the fi - re starts to mel - low,

© 1979 EMI APRIL MUSIC INC. and HICKORY GROVE MUSIC
All Rights Controlled and Administered by EMI APRIL MUSIC INC.
All Rights Reserved   International Copyright Secured   Used by Permission

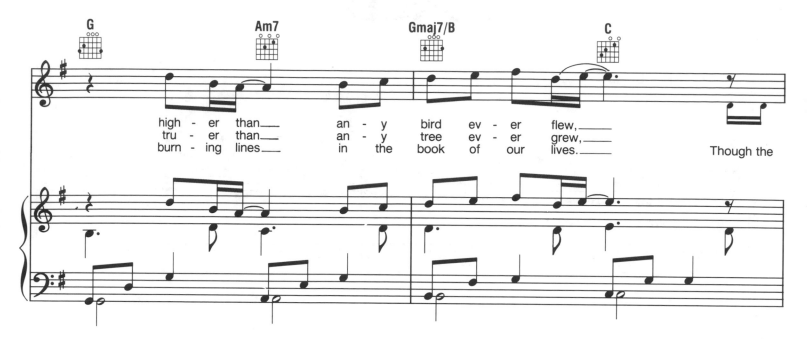

high - er than____ an - y bird ev - er flew,____
tru - er than____ an - y tree ev - er grew,____
burn - ing lines ____ in the book of our lives.____

Though the

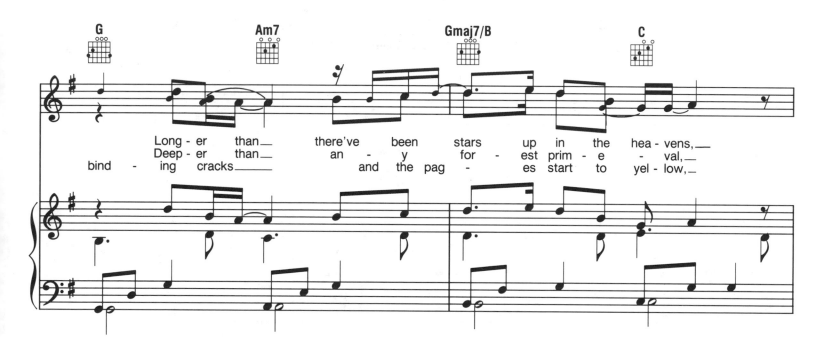

Long - er than____ there've been stars up in the hea - vens,____
Deep - er than____ an - y for - est prim - e - - val,____
bind - ing cracks____ and the pag - es start to yel - low,____

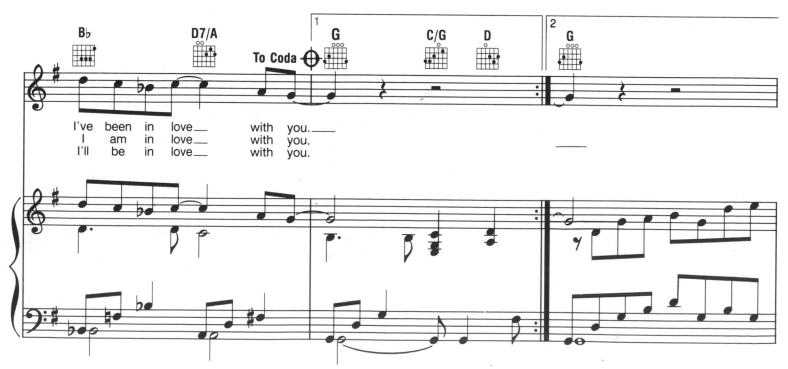

To Coda ⊕

I've been in love____ with you.____
I am in love____ with you.____
I'll be in love____ with you.

HOW CAN I FALL?

Words and Music by DAVID GLASPER, MARCUS LILLINGTON,
IAN SPICE and MICHAEL DELAHUNTY

Moderate Ballad

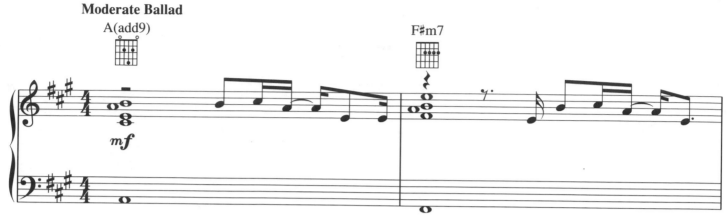

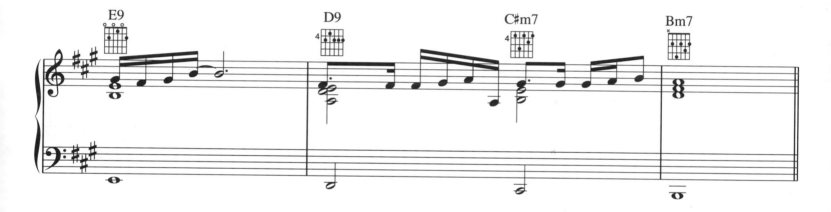

Give __ me time __ to care.   The mo - ment's here __ for us __ to share, __
Could __ I lie __ to you,   I'm just __ too weak __ to face __ the truth.
When __ all faith __ is gone,   I fight __ my - self __ to car - ry on. __
Now __ I hold __ this line.   I know __ the choice __ to leave __ is mine. __

© 1988 EMI VIRGIN MUSIC LTD.
All Rights Controlled and Administered in the U.S. and Canada by EMI VIRGIN MUSIC, INC.
All Rights Reserved   International Copyright Secured   Used by Permission

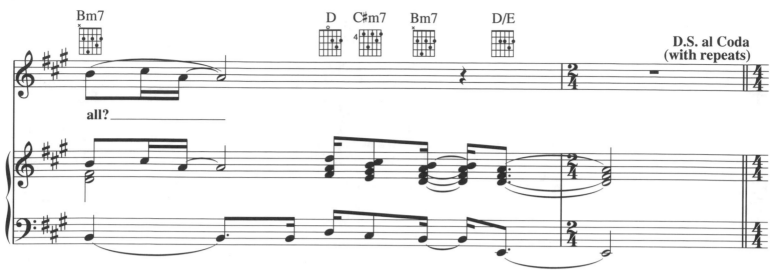

D.S. al Coda
(with repeats)

all?

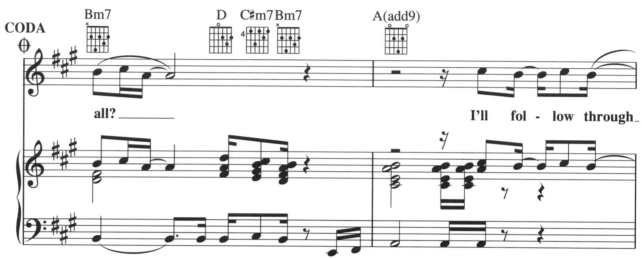

CODA

all?

I'll fol - low through

I'll see I do when the

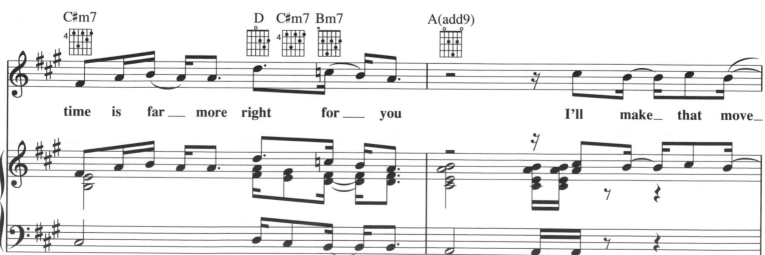

time is far more right for you

I'll make that move

KISSING A FOOL

Words and Music by
GEORGE MICHAEL

You are far
(See additional lyrics)
when I could have been _ your star

you lis - tened to peo - ple, who scared you to death and from my heart,

Copyright © 1987 by Morrison-Leahy Music Ltd.
All Rights for the U.S. Administered by Chappell & Co.
International Copyright Secured   All Rights Reserved

73

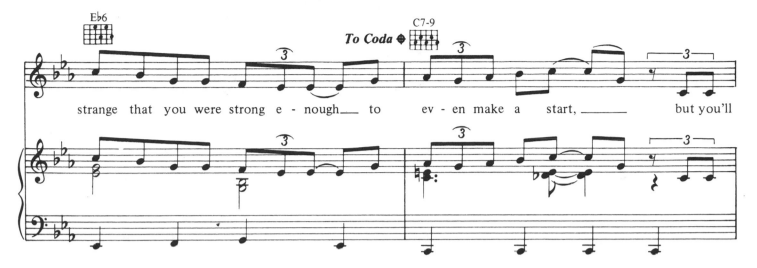

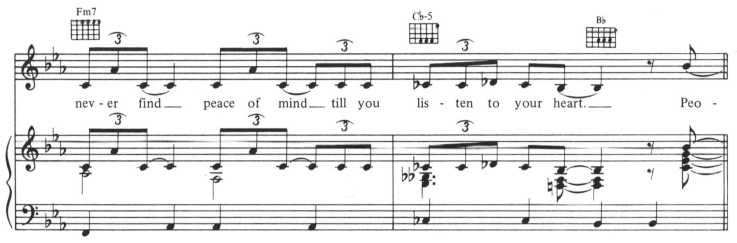

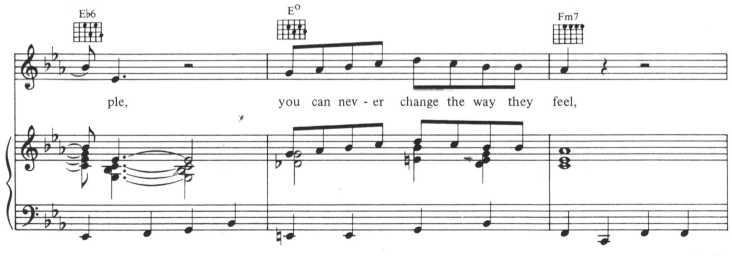

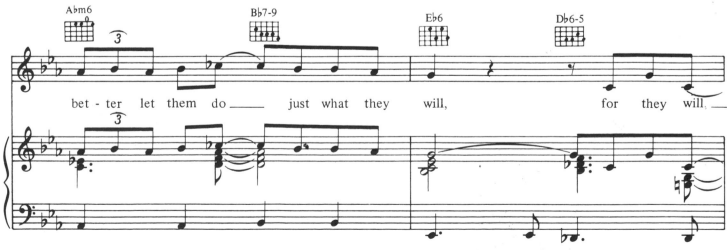

if you let them steal your heart from you. Peo-

ple, will al - ways make a lov - er

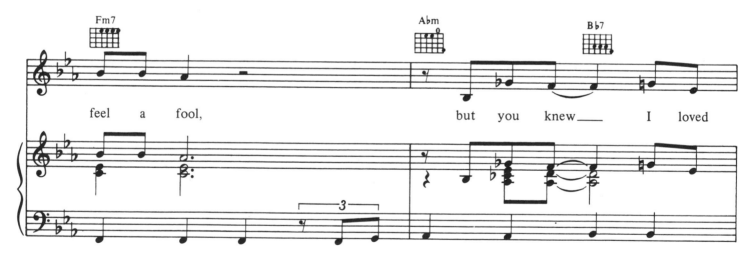

feel a fool, but you knew___ I loved

you we could have shown them all,_____ we

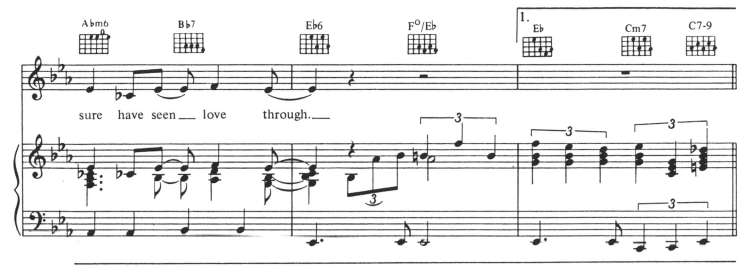

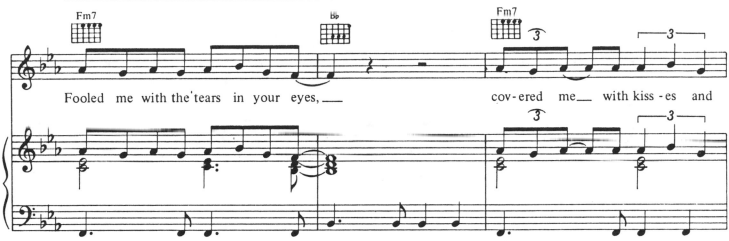

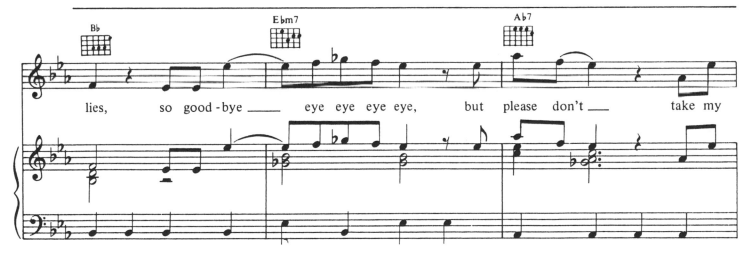

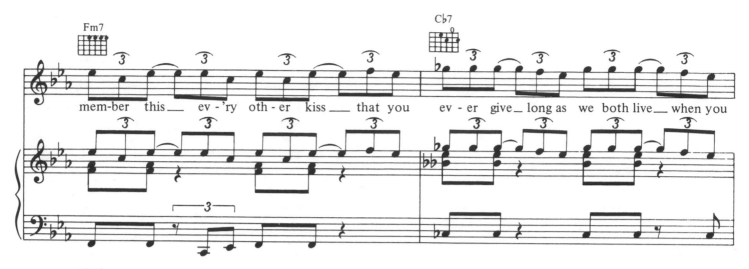

mem-ber this___ ev -'ry oth - er kiss___ that you ev - er give__ long as we both live__ when you

need the hand__ of an-oth - er man,__ one you real - ly can sur - ren-der with,__ I will

wait for you__ like I al - ways do,__ there's some - thing that,___ that

can't com - pare___ with an - y oth - er.___

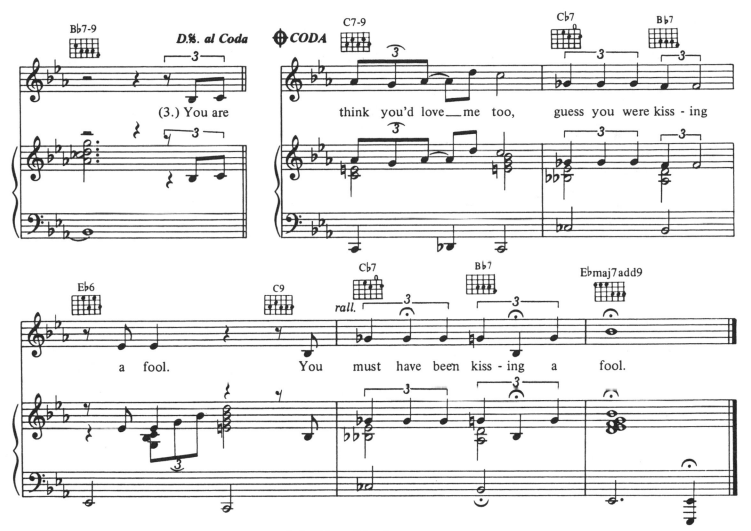

Additional lyrics

VERSE 2:
You are far
I'm never gonna be your star
I'll pick up the pieces and mend my heart
Maybe I'll be strong enough
I don't know where to start
But I'll never find peace of mind
While I listen to my heart.
People you can never change the way they feel
Better let them do just what they will
For they will
If you let them steal your heart.
People
Will always make a lover feel a fool
But you knew I loved you
We could have shown you all la la la la la la la.

VERSE 3:
You are far
When I could have been your star
You listened to people
Who scared you to death and from my heart
Strange that I was wrong enough
To think you'd love me too
Guess you were kissing a fool
You must have been kissing a fool.

LEADER OF THE BAND

Words and Music by
DAN FOGELBERG

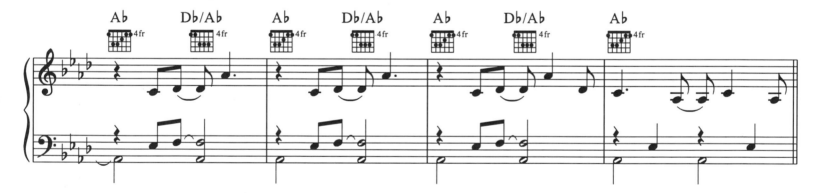

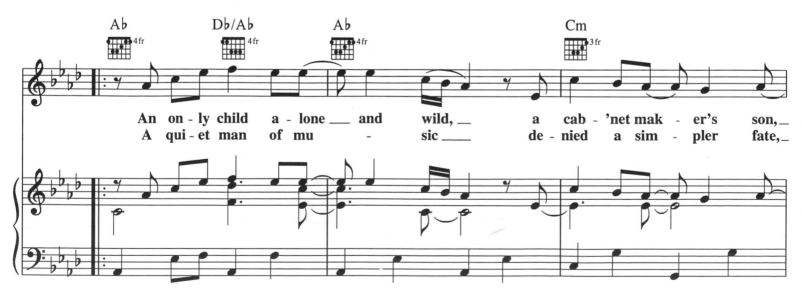

An on-ly child a-lone ___ and wild, ___ a cab-'net mak-er's son, ___
A qui-et man of mu - sic ___ de-nied a sim-pler fate, ___

© 1981 EMI APRIL MUSIC INC. and HICKORY GROVE MUSIC
All Rights Controlled and Administered by EMI APRIL MUSIC INC.
All Rights Reserved   International Copyright Secured   Used by Permission

My life has been a poor ___ at - tempt ___ to im - i - tate the man. ___

___ I'm just a liv - ing leg - a - cy ___ to the lead - er of ___ the

band.

My broth-er's lives were dif - f'rent for they heard an-oth-er call; ___
I thank you for the mu - sic and your sto - ries of the road. ___

83

nough.   The lead-er   of   the band __ is   tired __   and __ his

leg - a - cy ____ to the lead - er of _____ the

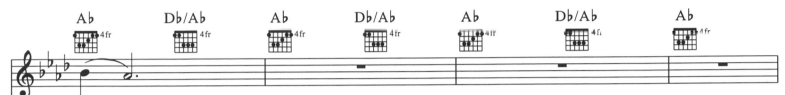

band. __

THE LONGEST TIME

Words and Music by
BILLY JOEL

Bright Rock and Roll, in 2

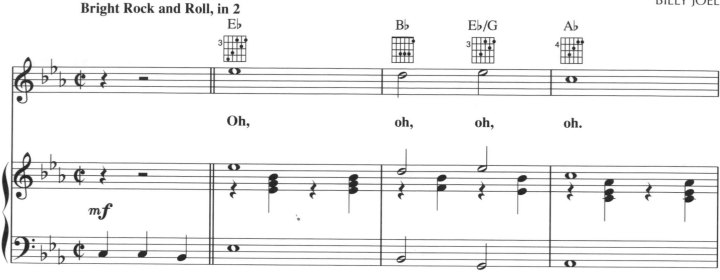

Oh, oh, oh, oh.

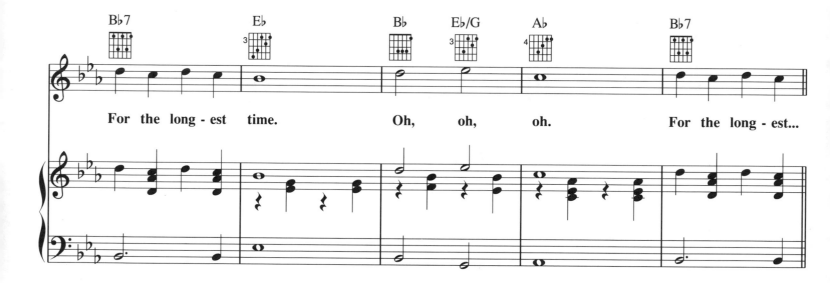

For the long-est time. Oh, oh, oh. For the long-est...

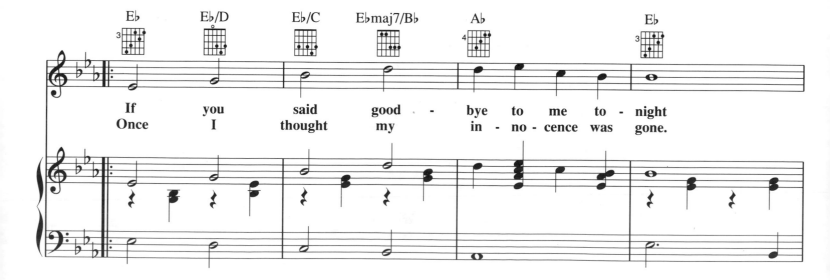

If you said good-bye to me to-night
Once I thought my in-no-cence was gone.

© 1983 JOEL SONGS
All Rights Controlled and Administered by EMI BLACKWOOD MUSIC INC.
All Rights Reserved   International Copyright Secured   Used by Permission

MAKE IT REAL

Words and Music by LINDA MALLAH,
RICK KELLY and DON POWELL

Copyright © 1987 Meow Baby Music, Careers-BMG Music Publishing, Inc. and Demerie Music
International Copyright Secured   All Rights Reserved

94

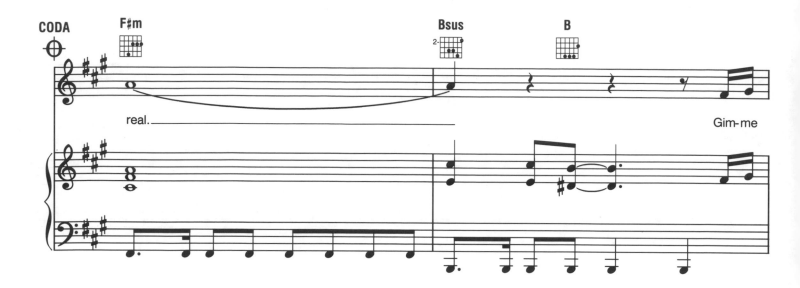

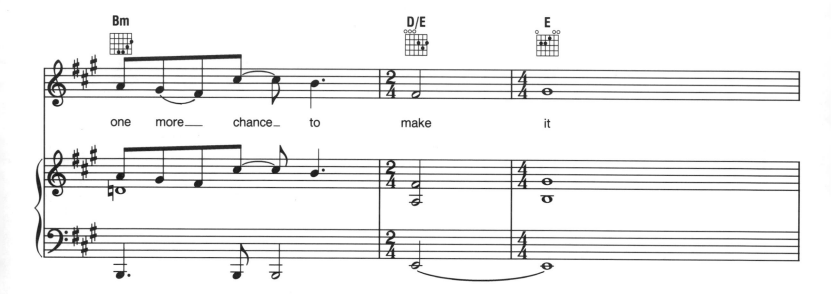

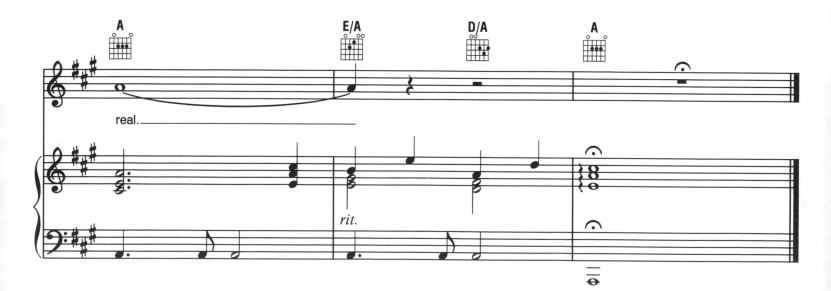

The Next Time I Fall

Words and Music by PAUL GORDON
and BOBBY CALDWELL

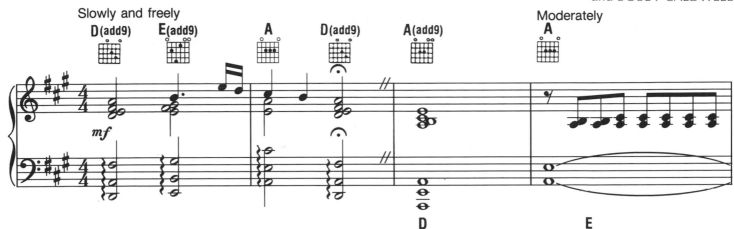

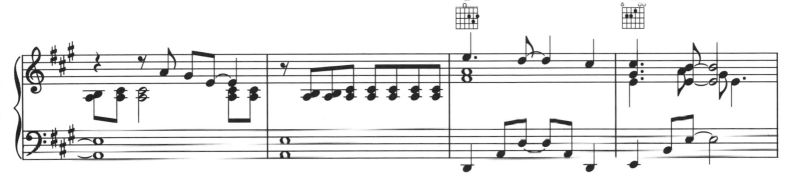

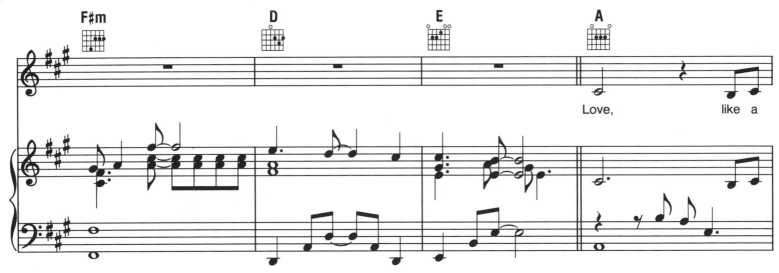

road that ne - ver ends.____ How it leads me back_ a - gain____ to

© 1986 EMI BLACKWOOD MUSIC INC., SIN-DROME MUSIC, CHAPPELL & CO. and FRENCH SURF MUSIC
All Rights for SIN-DROME MUSIC Controlled and Administered by EMI BLACKWOOD MUSIC INC.
All Rights for FRENCH SURF MUSIC Administered by CHAPPELL & CO.
All Rights Reserved   International Copyright Secured   Used by Permission

102

ONE

Words and Music by BARRY GIBB,
MAURICE GIBB and ROBIN GIBB

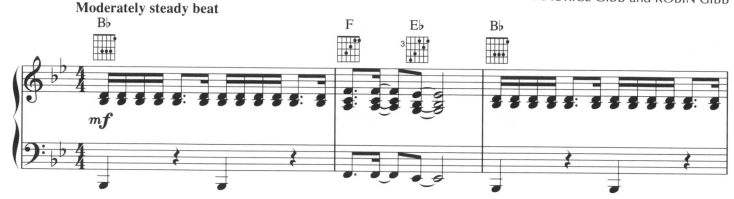

Moderately steady beat

I feel my heart _____ beat _____
stand- ing on _____ this cor - ner
fol - _____ low. _____

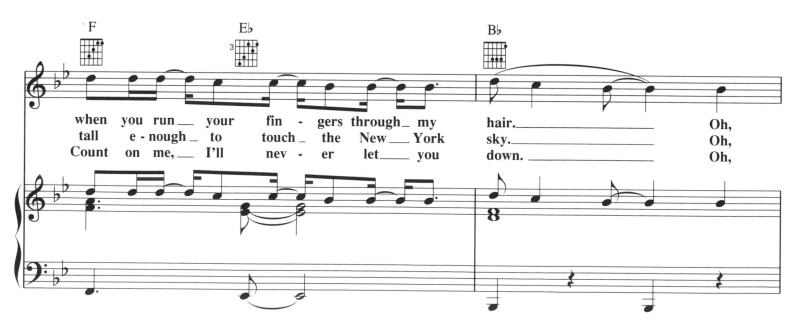

when you run _____ your fin - gers through _____ my hair. _____ Oh,
tall e - nough _____ to touch _____ the New _____ York sky. _____ Oh,
Count on me, _____ I'll nev - er let _____ you down. _____ Oh,

Copyright © 1989 by Gibb Brothers Music
All Rights Administered by Careers-BMG Music Publishing, Inc.
International Copyright Secured   All Rights Reserved

106

RIGHT HERE WAITING

Words and Music by
RICHARD MARX

Copyright © 1989 Chi-Boy Music (ASCAP)
International Copyright Secured   All Rights Reserved

113

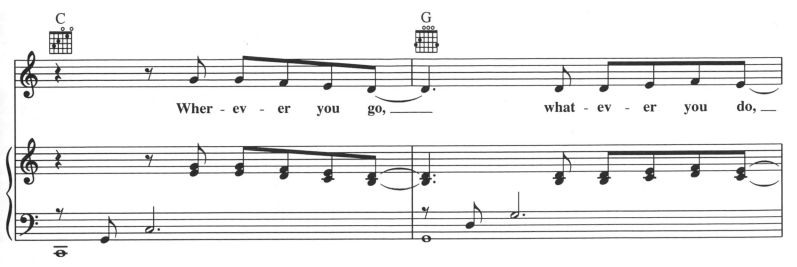

115

ONE MORE TRY

Words and Music by
GEORGE MICHAEL

(1.) I've had e-nough of dan - ger, and peo-ple on _ the streets, _

[2°] [bye.]
(See additional lyrics)

I'm look-ing out for an - gels, just trying to find_ some_peace.

Copyright © 1987 by Morrison-Leahy Music Ltd.
All Rights in the U.S. Administered by Chappell & Co.
International Copyright Secured All Rights Reserved

I know you're wrong, you're not that strong, let me go. _____

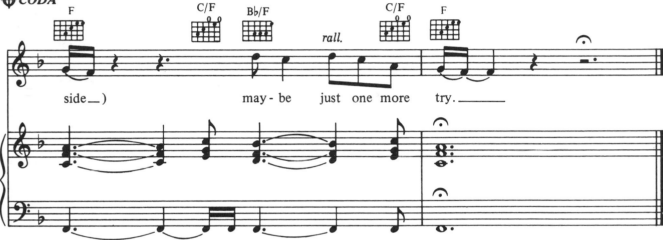

side __) may - be just one more try. _____

Additional lyrics

VERSE 2:

When you were just a stranger
And I was at your feet
I didn't feel the danger
Now I feel the heat
That look in your eyes
Telling me no
So you think that you love me
Know that you need me
I wrote the song, I know it's wrong
Just let me go . . .

D.S.

And teacher
There are things
That I still have to learn
But the one thing I have is my pride
Oh so I don't want to learn to
Hold you, touch you
Think that you're mine
Because there ain't no joy
For an uptown boy
Who just isn't willing to try
I'm so cold
Inside.

SAVING ALL MY LOVE FOR YOU

Words by GERRY GOFFIN
Music by MICHAEL MASSER

© 1978 SCREEN GEMS-EMI MUSIC INC., LAUREN-WESLEY MUSIC INC. and PRINCE STREET MUSIC
All Rights for LAUREN-WESLEY MUSIC INC. Controlled and Administered by SCREEN GEMS-EMI MUSIC INC.
All Rights Reserved   International Copyright Secured   Used by Permission

SEPARATE LIVES
(Love Theme From "WHITE NIGHTS")

Words and Music by
STEPHEN BISHOP

Copyright © 1985 by Stephen Bishop Music Publishing Company, Gold Horizon Music Corp. and Hit & Run Music Publishing Ltd.
All Rights for Stephen Bishop Music Publishing Company Administered by Careers-BMG Music Publishing, Inc.
International Copyright Secured   All Rights Reserved

sep - 'rate lives.

Well, I held on

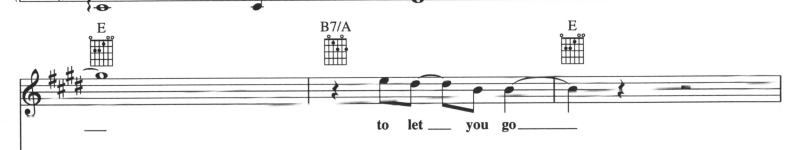

to let ___ you go

and if you lost ___ your love ___ for me ___ will you nev - er let it

THROUGH THE YEARS

Words and Music by STEVE DORFF
and MARTY PANZER

Appreciatively

I can't re-mem-ber when
can't re-mem-ber what

you were-n't there
I used to do

When I did-n't care for
Who I trust-ed Who I

an-y-one but you
list-ened to be-fore

I swear we've been through ev-ery-thing there is
I swear you've taught me ev-ery-thing I know

Copyright © 1980 by Careers-BMG Music Publishing, Inc. and SwaneeBRAVO! Music
International Copyright Secured   All Rights Reserved

Can't im-a-gine an-y-thing___ we've missed   Can't im-a-gine an-y-thing___ the
Can't im-a-gine need-ing some-one___ so___   But Through The Years it seems   to me___   I

two   of us___ can't   do   Through The   Years   You've ne-ver   let me
need you more___ and more___   Through The   Years   Through all   the good and

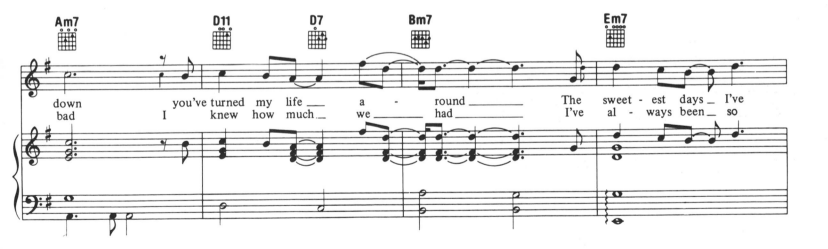

down   you've turned my life___ a - round_____   The sweet-est days___ I've
bad   I   knew how much___ we_____ had_____   I've al - ways been so

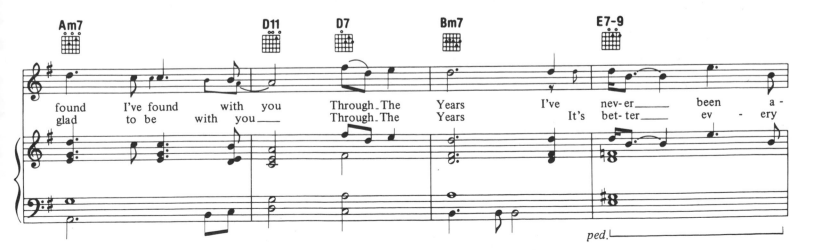

found   I've found   with you   Through_The   Years   I've nev-er_____ been a-
glad   to be   with you___   Through_The   Years   It's bet-ter_____ ev - ery

*ped.*_____

TRULY

Words and Music by
LIONEL RICHIE

Copyright © 1982 Brockman Music (ASCAP)
International Copyright Secured   All Rights Reserved

WOMAN IN LOVE

Words and Music by BARRY GIBB
and ROBIN GIBB

Moderately Slow

Life is a mo-ment in space,___ when the dream is gone___ it's a lone-li-er place.___
With you e-ter-nal-ly mine,___ in love there is___ no meas-ure of time.___

Copyright © 1980 by Gibb Brothers Music
All Rights Administered by Careers-BMG Music Publishing, Inc.
International Copyright Secured   All Rights Reserved

THESE DREAMS

Words and Music by MARTIN PAGE
and TAUPIN

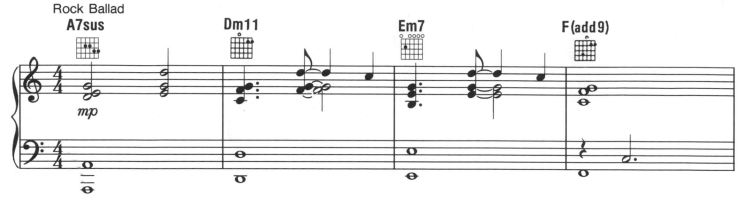

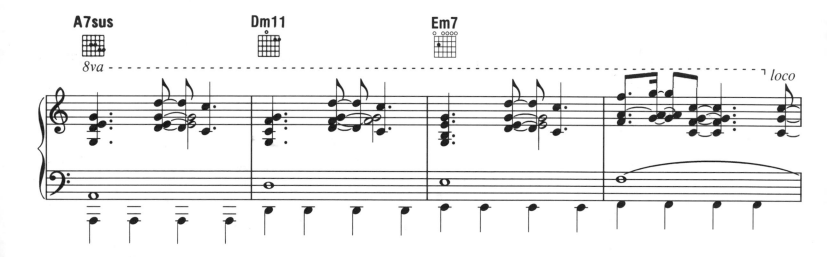

Spare a lit-tle can-dle, save___ some light for me;___
Is it cloak___ and dag-ger, could___ it be spring or fall?___
The sweet-est song___ is si-lence that___ I've ev-er heard.___

Copyright © 1985 by Little Mole Music and Zomba Music Publishers Ltd.
All Rights for Little Mole Music Administered by Intersong U.S.A., Inc.
All Rights for Zomba Music Publishers Ltd. Controlled by Zomba Enterprises, Inc. for the U.S.A. and Canada
International Copyright Secured   All Rights Reserved

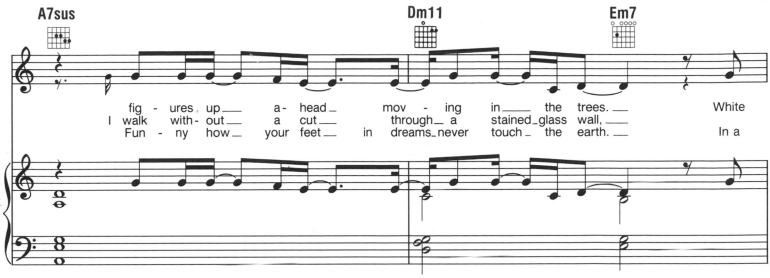

figures up a-head moving in the trees. White
I walk with-out a cut through a stained glass wall,
Fun-ny how your feet in dreams never touch the earth. In a

skin in lin-en, per-fume on my wrist, and a
weak-er in my eye-sight, can-dle in my grip, and
wood full of princ-es free-dom is a kiss, but the

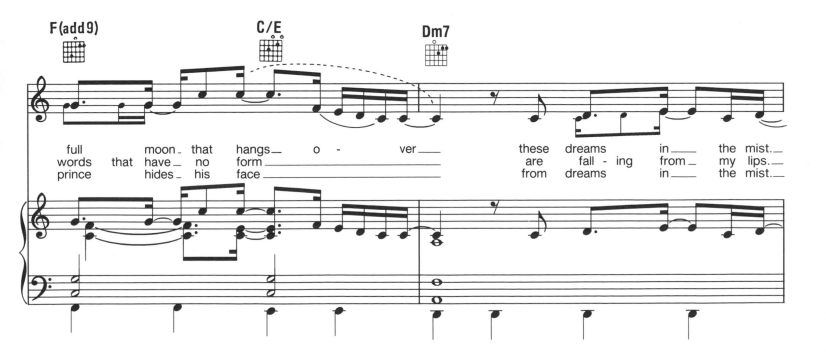

full moon that hangs o - ver these dreams in the mist.
words that have no form are fall-ing from my lips.
prince hides his face from dreams in the mist.

The Greatest Songs Ever Written

The Best Ever Collection

Arranged for Piano, Voice & Guitar

150 Of The Most Beautiful Songs Ever

Over 400 pages of slow and sentimental ballads, including: Come In From The Rain • Edelweiss • The First Time Ever I Saw Your Face • For All We Know • How Deep Is Your Love • I Have Dreamed • I'll Be Seeing You • If We Only Have Love • Love Is Blue • Red Roses For A Blue Lady • Songbird • Summertime • Unchained Melody • Yesterday, When I Was Young • Young At Heart • many more.
00360735 ....$19.95

The Best Big Band Songs Ever

69 of the greatest big band songs ever, including: Ballin' The Jack • Basin Street Blues • Boogie Woogie Bugle Boy • The Continental • Don't Get Around Much Anymore • In The Mood • Let A Smile Be Your Umbrella • Marie • Moonglow • Opus One • Satin Doll • Sentimental Journey • String Of Pearls • Who's Sorry Now.
00359129 ....$15.95

The Best Broadway Songs Ever

Over 65 songs in all! Highlights include: All I Ask Of You • As Long As He Needs Me • Bess, You Is My Woman • Bewitched • Camelot • Climb Ev'ry Mountain • Comedy Tonight • Don't Cry For Me Argentina • Everything's Coming Up Roses • Getting To Know You • I Could Have Danced All Night • I Dreamed A Dream • If I Were A Rich Man • The Last Night Of The World • Love Changes Everything • Oklahoma! • Ol' Man River • People • Try To Remember • and many more!
00309155 ....$16.95

The Best Christmas Songs Ever

Newly Revised!
A collection of 72 of the most-loved songs of the season, including: Blue Christmas • The Chipmunk Song • Frosty The Snow Man • A Holly Jolly Christmas • Home For The Holidays • I'll Be Home For Christmas • Jingle-Bell Rock • Let It Snow! Let It Snow! Let It Snow! • Parade Of The Wooden Soldiers • Rudolph, The Red-Nosed Reindeer • Santa, Bring Back My Baby (To Me) • Silver Bells • Suzy Snowflake • Toyland.
00359130 ....$16.95

The Best Country Songs Ever

Over 65 songs, featuring: Always On My Mind • Behind Closed Doors • Could I Have This Dance • Crazy • Daddy Sang Bass • D-I-V-O-R-C-E • Forever And Ever, Amen • God Bless The U.S.A. • Grandpa (Tell Me 'Bout The Good Old Days) • Help Me Make It Through The Night • I Fall To Pieces • Mammas Don't Let Your Babies Grow Up To Be Cowboys • Stand By Your Man • Through The Years • and more.
00359135 ....$16.95

The Best Easy Listening Songs Ever

A collection of 75 mellow favorites, featuring: All Out Of Love • Can't Smile Without You • (They Long To Be) Close To You • Every Breath You Take • Eye In The Sky • How Am I Supposed To Live Without You • I Dreamed A Dream • Imagine • Love Takes Time • Piano Man • The Rainbow Connection • Sing • Vision Of Love • Your Song.
00359193 ....$15.95

The Best Jazz Standards Ever

77 of the greatest jazz hits of all time, including: April In Paris • Body And Soul • Don't Get Around Much Anymore • I Got It Bad And That Ain't Good • I've Got You Under My Skin • It Don't Mean A Thing (If It Ain't Got That Swing) • Love Is Here To Stay • Misty • Out Of Nowhere • Satin Doll • Unforgettable • When I Fall In Love • and many more.
00311641 ....$17.95

The Best Love Songs Ever

A collection of 66 favorite love songs, including: The Anniversary Song • (They Long To Be) Close To You • Endless Love • Here And Now • Just The Way You Are • Longer • Love Takes Time • Misty • My Funny Valentine • So In Love • You Needed Me • Your Song.
00359198 ....$15.95

The Best Rock Songs Ever

70 songs, including: All Day And All Of The Night • All Shook Up • Ballroom Blitz • Bennie And The Jets • Blue Suede Shoes • Born To Be Wild • Boys Are Back In Town • Every Breath You Take • Faith • Free Bird • Hey Jude • Lola • Louie, Louie • Maggie May • Money • (She's) Some Kind Of Wonderful • Takin' Care Of Business • Walk This Way • We Didn't Start The Fire • We Got The Beat • Wild Thing • more!
00490424 ....$16.95

The Best Songs Ever

76 songs in all, featuring: All I Ask Of You • Cabaret • Can't Smile Without You • Candle In The Wind • Do-Re-Mi • Don't Know Much • Feelings • Fly Me To The Moon • The Girl From Ipanema • Here's That Rainy Day • I Can't Help Falling In Love • I Left My Heart In San Francisco • I Write The Songs • Imagine • In The Mood • Let It Be Me • Longer • Love On The Rocks • More • My Way • People • Send In The Clowns • Some Enchanted Evening • Somewhere Out There • Stormy Weather • Strangers In The Night • Sunrise, Sunset • What A Wonderful World.
00359224 ....$17.95

The Best Standards Ever

Volume 1 (A-L)
72 beautiful ballads, including: All The Things You Are • Bewitched • Can't Help Lovin' Dat Man • Don't Get Around Much Anymore • Getting To Know You • God Bless' The Child • Hello, Young Lovers • I Got It Bad And That Ain't Good • It's Only A Paper Moon • I've Got You Under My Skin • The Lady Is A Tramp • Little White Lies.
00359231 ....$15.95

Volume 2 (M-Z)
72 songs, including: Makin' Whoopee • Misty • Moonlight In Vermont • My Funny Valentine • Old Devil Moon • The Party's Over • People Will Say We're In Love • Smoke Gets In Your Eyes • Strangers In The Night • Tuxedo Junction • Yesterday.
00359232 ....$15.95

FOR MORE INFORMATION, SEE YOUR LOCAL MUSIC DEALER, OR WRITE TO:

HAL•LEONARD™
CORPORATION
7777 W. BLUEMOUND RD. P.O. BOX 13819 MILWAUKEE, WI 53213

Prices, contents and availability subject to change without notice. Not all products available outside the U.S.A.